W9-CFB-440

Reptiles

# Bearded Dragons

by Lyn A. Sirota

Consulting Editor: Gail Saunders-Smith, PhD
Content Consultants: Joe Maierhauser, President/CEO
Terry Phillip, Curator of Reptiles
Reptile Gardens, Rapid City, South Dakota

Capstone press

Mankato, Minnesota

Pebble Plus is published by Capstone Press,
151 Good Counsel Drive, P.O. Box 669, Mankato, Minnesota 56002.
*www.capstonepress.com*

Books published by Capstone Press are manufactured with paper
containing at least 10 percent post-consumer waste.

*Library of Congress Cataloging-in-Publication Data*
Sirota, Lyn A., 1963–
    Bearded dragons / by Lyn A. Sirota.
    p. cm. — (Pebble plus. Reptiles)
    Includes bibliographical references and index.
    Summary: "Simple text and photographs present bearded dragons,
how they look, where they live, and what they do" — Provided by publisher.
    ISBN 978-1-4296-3319-2 (library binding)
    1. Bearded dragons (Reptiles) — Juvenile literature. I. Title.
SF459.L5S57 2010
597.95'5 — dc22                              2009000040

**Editorial Credits**
Jenny Marks, editor; Matt Bruning, designer; Svetlana Zhurkin, photo researcher

**Photo Credits**
Alamy/Juniors Bildarchiv, 15
Minden Pictures/Michael & Patricia Fogden, 9; Patricio Robles Gil, 7
Photolibrary/Oxford Scientific/Emanuele Biggi, 13
Shutterstock/Ashley Whitworth, 5; Audrey Snider-Bell, cover; Brooke Whatnall, cover, 11; clearviewstock, 1; Eric
    Gevaert, 17; Ramon Grosso Dolarea, 19

# Note to Parents and Teachers

The Pebble Plus Reptiles set supports science standards related to life science. This book
describes and illustrates bearded dragons. The images support early readers in understanding
the text. The repetition of words and phrases helps early readers learn new words. This book
also introduces early readers to subject-specific vocabulary words, which are defined in the
Glossary section. Early readers may need assistance to read some words and to use the Table of
Contents, Glossary, Read More, Internet Sites, and Index sections of the book.

# Table of Contents

# Puffy Pouches

Bearded dragons are lizards.

Their pointy beards

are really throat pouches.

Bearded dragons puff out

their pouches with air.

Bearded dragons can be up to 2 feet (.6 meter) long. Spines cover their pouches and bodies.

# Deserts and Woods

Bearded dragons live in deserts
and forests in Australia.
They climb trees and bushes.

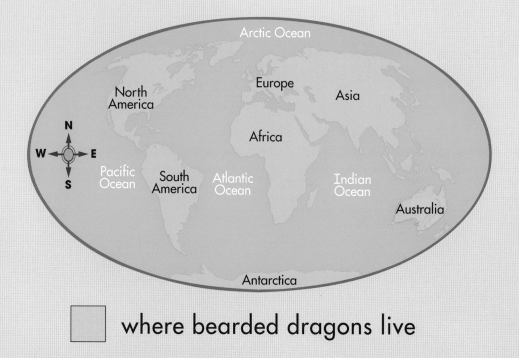

where bearded dragons live

To keep warm, bearded dragons
sit on sunny tree branches.
Resting under sand and dirt
keeps them cool.

# Dragon Talk

Male bearded dragons

bob their heads.

Bobbing tells other lizards

they are in charge.

Bearded dragons stand
and wave a front leg.
They are warning
other lizards to stay away.

# Eat or Be Eaten

Bearded dragons
are not picky eaters.
They live where
there is little food.
Any bug or plant will do.

If a predator grabs

a bearded dragon's tail,

the tail breaks off.

The tailless lizard runs away.

In time, the tail grows back.

# Life Cycle

Female bearded dragons

lay about 24 eggs in nests.

After about 70 days,

the lizards hatch.

They live up to 10 years.

# Bearded Dragon Life Cycle

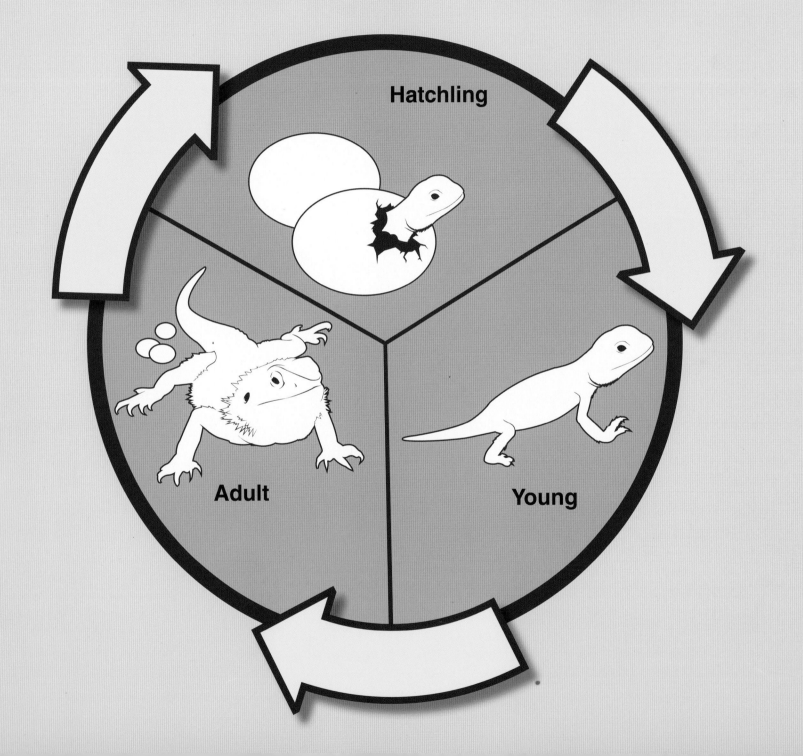

Hatchling

Young

Adult

# Glossary

**bob** — to move up and down

**desert** — a sandy land in hot places

**hatch** — to break out of an egg

**pouch** — a small pocket of skin; bearded lizards have throat pouches.

**predator** — an animal that hunts other animals for food

**spine** — a sharp pointy growth on the body of a lizard

# Read More

**Bredeson, Carmen**. *Fun Facts about Reptiles.* I Like Reptiles and Amphibians! Berkeley, N.J.: Enslow, 2008.

**Glaser, Jason**. *Bearded Dragons.* World of Reptiles. Mankato, Minn.: Capstone Press, 2007.

**Sirota, Lyn A**. *Horned Lizards.* Reptiles. Mankato, Minn.: Capstone Press, 2010.

# Internet Sites

FactHound offers a safe, fun way to find Internet sites related to this book. All of the sites on FactHound have been researched by our staff.

Here's all you do:

Visit *www.facthound.com*

FactHound will fetch the best sites for you!

# Index

Word Count: 162
Grade: 1
Early-Intervention Level: 20